FAITH LESSONS

ON THE

promised

LAND

CROSSROADS of THE WORLD

PARTICIPANT'S GUIDE

Also available from Ray Vander Laan

Video and Curriculum

Faith Lessons on the Death and Resurrection of the Messiah
Faith Lessons on the Life and Ministry of the Messiah
Faith Lessons on the Prophets and Kings of Israel

Book and Audiocassette

Echoes of His Presence

CD-ROM

Jesus: An Interactive Journey

FAITH LESSONS
ON THE
promised
LAND
CROSSROADS OF THE WORLD

PARTICIPANT'S GUIDE

Ray Vander Laan

with
Stephen and Amanda Sorenson

GRAND RAPIDS, MICHIGAN 49530

ZONDERVAN™

Faith Lessons on the Promised Land Participant's Guide

Copyright © 1999 by Ray Vander Laan

Requests for information should be addressed to:

Zondervan, *Grand Rapids, Michigan 49530*

ISBN 0-310-67896-X

Interior design by Sherri Hoffman

Printed in the United States of America

06 07 08 09 10 • 28 27 26 25 24 23 22 21

contents

Introduction

Because God speaks to us through the Scriptures, studying them is a rewarding experience. The inspired human authors of the Bible, as well as those to whom the words were originally given, were primarily Jews living in the Near East. God's words and actions spoke to them with such power, clarity, and purpose that they wrote them down and carefully preserved them as an authoritative body of literature.

God's use of human servants in revealing Himself resulted in writings that clearly bear the stamp of time and place. The message of the Scriptures is, of course, eternal and unchanging—but the circumstances and conditions of the people of the Bible are unique to their times. Consequently, we most clearly understand God's truth when we know the cultural context within which He spoke and acted and the perception of the people with whom He communicated. This does not mean that God's revelation is unclear if we don't know the cultural context. Rather, by learning how to think and approach life as Abraham, Moses, Ruth, Esther, and Paul did, modern Christians will deepen their appreciation of God's Word. To fully apply the message of the Bible, we must enter the world of the Hebrews and familiarize ourselves with their culture.

That is the purpose of this study. The events and characters of the Bible are presented in their original settings. Although the videos offer the latest archaeological research, this series is not intended to be a definitive cultural and geographical study of the lands of the Bible. No original scientific discoveries are revealed here. The purpose of this study is to help us better understand God's revealed mission for our lives by enabling us to hear and see His words in their original context.

understanding the world of the Hebrews

More than 3,800 years ago, God spoke to His servant Abraham: "Go, walk through the length and breadth of the land, for I am giving it to you" (Genesis 13:17). From the outset, God's choice of a Hebrew nomad to begin His plan of salvation (that is still unfolding) was linked to the selection of a specific land where His redemptive work would begin. The nature of God's covenant relationship with His people demanded a place where their faith could be exercised and displayed to all nations so that the world would know of *Yahweh*, the true and faithful God. God showed the same care in preparing a land for His chosen people as He did in preparing a people to live in that land. For us to fully understand God's plan and purpose for His people, we must first understand the nature of the place He selected for them.

By New Testament times, the Jewish people had been removed from the Promised Land by the Babylonians due to Israel's failure to live obediently before God (Jeremiah 25:4–11). The exile lasted seventy years, but its impact upon God's people was astounding. New patterns of worship developed, and scribes and experts in God's law shaped the new commitment to be faithful to Him. The prophets predicted the appearance of a Messiah like King David who would revive the kingdom of the Hebrew people.

But the Promised Land was now home to many other groups of people whose religious practices, moral values, and lifestyles conflicted with those of the Jews. Living as God's witnesses took on added difficulty as Greek, Roman, and Samaritan worldviews mingled with that of the Israelites. The Promised Land was divided between kings and governors, usually under the authority of one foreign empire or another. But the mission of God's people did not change. They were still to live *so that the world would know that their God was the true God.* And the land continued to provide them opportunity to encounter the world that desperately needed to know this reality.

The Promised Land was the arena within which God's people were to serve Him faithfully as the world watched. The land God chose for His people was on the crossroads of the world. A major trade route, the Via Maris, ran through it. God intended for the Israelites to take control of the cities along this route and thereby exert influence on the nations around them. Through their righteous living, the Hebrews were to reveal the one true God, *Yahweh,* to the world. They failed to accomplish this mission, however, because of their unfaithfulness.

Western Christianity tends to spiritualize the concept of the Promised Land as it is presented in the Bible. Instead of seeing it as a crossroads from which to influence the world, modern Christians view it as a distant, heavenly city, a glorious "Canaan" toward which we are traveling as we ignore the world around us. We are focused on the destination, not the journey. We have unconsciously separated our walk with God from our responsibility to the world in which He has placed us. In one sense, our earthly experience is simply preparation for an eternity in the "promised land." Preoccupation with this idea, however, distorts the mission God has set for us.

Living by faith is not a vague, otherworldly experience; rather, it is being faithful to God right now, in the place and time in which He has put us. This truth is emphasized by God's choice of Canaan, a crossroads of the ancient world, as the Promised Land for the Israelites. God wants His people to be in the game, not on the bench. Our mission, as Christians today, is the same one He gave to the Israelites. We are to live obediently *within* the world so that through us *the world may know that our God is the one true God.*

The Assumptions of Biblical Writers

Biblical writers assumed that their readers were familiar with Near Eastern geography. The geography of Canaan shaped the culture of the people living there. Their settlements began near sources of water and food. Climate and raw materials shaped their choice of occupation, dress, weapons, diet, and even artistic expression. As their cities grew, they interacted politically. Trade developed, and trade routes were established.

During New Testament times, the Promised Land was called Palestine or Judea. *Judea* (which means "Jewish") technically referred to the land that had been the nation of Judah. Because of the influence that the people of Judea had over the rest of the land, the land itself was called Judea. The Romans divided the land into several provinces, including Judea, Samaria, and Galilee (the three main divisions during Jesus' time); Gaulanitis, the Decapolis, and Perea (east of the Jordan River); and Idumaea (Edom) and Nabatea (in the south). These further divisions of Israel added to the rich historical and cultural background God prepared for the coming of Jesus and the beginning of His church.

Today the names *Israel* and *Palestine* are often used to designate the land God gave to Abraham. Both terms are politically charged. *Palestine* is used by the Arabs living in the central part of the country, while *Israel* is used by the Jews to indicate the State of Israel. In this study, *Israel* is used in the biblical sense. This choice does not indicate a political statement regarding the current struggle in the Middle East but instead is chosen to best reflect the biblical designation for the land.

Unfortunately, many Christians do not have even a basic geographical knowledge of the region. This series is designed to help solve that problem. We will be studying the people and events of the Bible in their geographical and historical contexts. Once we know the *who*, *what*, and *where* of a Bible story, we will be able to understand the *why*. By deepening our understanding of God's Word, we can strengthen our relationship with God.

The biblical writers also used a language that, like all languages, is bound by culture and time. Therefore, understanding the Scriptures involves more than knowing what the words mean. We need to also understand those words from the perspective of the people who used them.

The people whom God chose as His instruments—the people to whom He revealed Himself—were Hebrews living in the Near East. These people described their world and themselves in concrete terms. Their language was one of pictures, metaphors, and examples rather than ideas, definitions, and abstractions. Whereas we might describe God as omniscient or omnipresent (knowing everything and present everywhere), a Hebrew would have preferred to describe God by saying, "The Lord is my shepherd." Thus, the Bible is filled with concrete images from Hebrew culture: God is our Father, and we are His children; God is the potter, and we are the clay; Jesus is the Lamb killed on Passover; heaven is an oasis in the desert, and hell is the city sewage dump; the Last Judgment will be in the Eastern Gate of the heavenly Jerusalem and will include sheep and goats.

These people had an Eastern mindset rather than a Western mindset. Eastern thought emphasizes the process of learning as much or more than the end result. Whereas Westerners tend to collect information to find the right answer, Hebrew thought stresses the process of discovery as well as the answer. So as you go through this study, use it as an opportunity to deepen your understanding of who God is and to grow in your relationship with Him.

standing at the crossroads

questions to think about

1. Think for a moment about where you live, what you do, and the people with whom you have contact. Can you think of specific reasons why God might have placed you where you are?

2. Remember when you have faced a difficult decision or resolved a crisis at a key crossroads in your life. Now imagine that another person is facing a similar challenge. If you had had the opportunity, what might you have left behind that would help that person benefit from your experience?

3. In what ways can we as Christians exert more influence on our culture and help people discover God?

video notes

Tel Gezer: Crossroads of the World

City Gates

Standing Stones

video нighlights

Look at the map of Israel below and locate Gezer.

1. What is so significant about Tel Gezer's location?

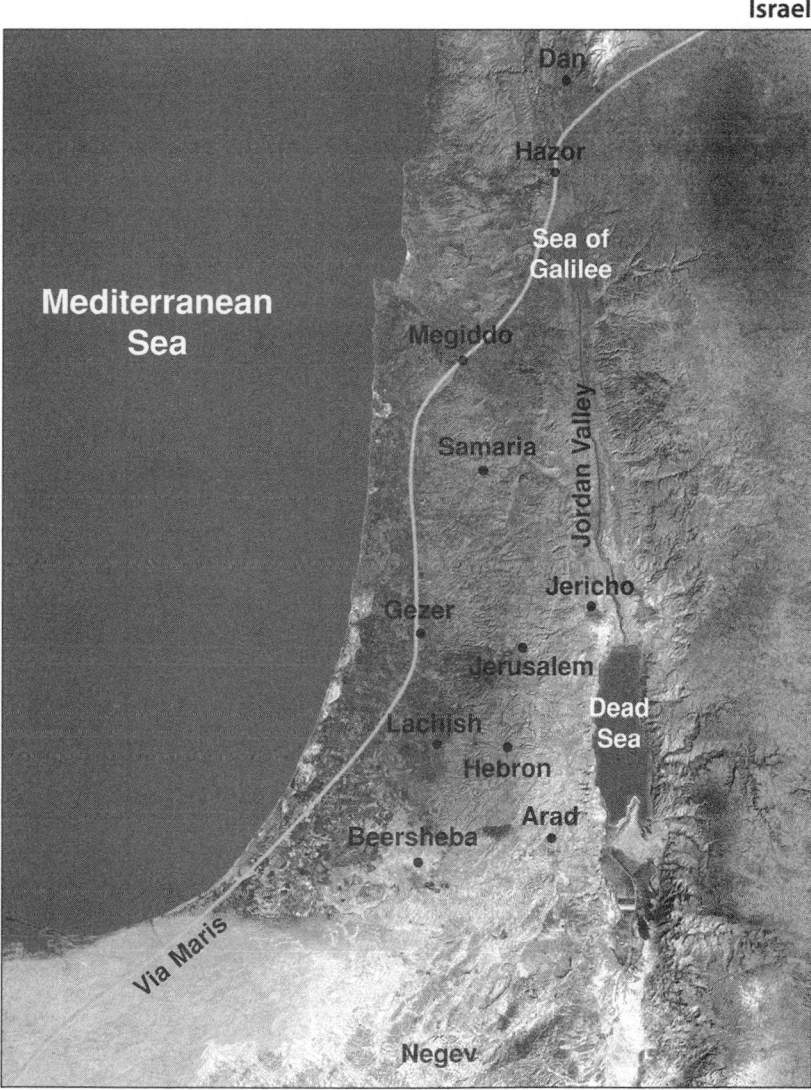

2. What did God intend to accomplish by choosing the land of Israel as the place where His people would live? What did the Israelites do that diminished the effectiveness of God's plan?

3. What new information or insight about city gates did you gain from the video?

4. What are "standing stones," and why were they erected?

THE TRUTH OF THE MATTER

Even though the Israelites seldom inhabited Gezer, and thus allowed the Canaanites to wield a much greater influence on the world's culture than they otherwise would have, the Canaanites living there did not have an easy life. In fact, the people of Gezer had a rough life. Consider:

- When Joshua led the Israelites into Canaan, Horam—the king of Gezer—attacked them, but Horam and his troops were all killed (Joshua 10:33).
- The tribe of Ephraim allowed the Canaanites to continue living in Gezer, but they used them as forced labor (Joshua 16:10).
- Pharaoh, king of Egypt, attacked and captured Gezer and then set it on fire. He killed its Canaanite inhabitants and gave it as a wedding gift to his daughter, Solomon's wife (1 Kings 9:16).
- During King David's reign, the Israelites battled the Philistines at Gezer (1 Chronicles 20:4). Years later, Solomon rebuilt Gezer's walls (including its huge, six-chambered gate) using forced laborers (1 Kings 9:15–17a).

small Group Bible Discovery

Topic A: God Carries Out His Plans

The Bible, especially the Old Testament, teaches that God is "sovereign"—in absolute control of all things. He has the power and patience to carry out through human history everything He has planned and promised to do.

1. Who did God choose to be the founder of Israel, and what did God promise to do? (See Genesis 12:1–3.)

2. What plot did Haman plan for the Jews, and how did God plan to use Esther—the Jewish queen of the King of Persia? (See Esther 3:1–6, 13; 4:1, 5–14.)

3. At times, God's plans seem doomed to failure. One such instance was during King Hezekiah's reign when King Sennacherib of Assyria threatened to destroy Jerusalem. Read Isaiah 37:15–22, 26, 32–36. In light of God's plan to make Himself known to the world, which significant truths are revealed in the following verses?

16	
17	
18–19	
20	

26	
32–34	
35	

4. What does Galatians 4:4–5 reveal about God's plan of salvation?

Topic B: God's Plan for His People

1. What did God, speaking through the prophet Isaiah, say that His people were to be? (See Isaiah 43:10–13.)

2. What, according to Solomon, was the reason God's people were to obey Him? (See 1 Kings 8:56–60.)

3. In each of the following Scriptures, what motivated the key person in the story?

Joshua 4:19–24	
1 Kings 18:21, 36–39	
Matthew 15:29–31	

4. What do the words of Rahab, the prostitute in Jericho who protected the spies of Israel, reveal about the effectiveness of God's plan when His people fulfill their part? (See Joshua 2:8–11.)

Topic C: City Gates

During biblical times, the city gate protected the entrance to the city and also functioned as the "city hall." So rulers, judges, or other officials "sat in the gate."

City Gates

1. Look up each of the following Scriptures and note what you learn about the people and their function in relationship to the city gates.

   a. Genesis 13:10–13; 18:20–21; 19:1, 9

   b. Deuteronomy 21:18–21

   c. Ruth 4:1–11

   d. 1 Samuel 4:10–18

   e. 2 Samuel 18:1–5; 19:1–8

   f. Esther 2:5–8, 19–23

DATA FILE

The Important Role of City Gates

During biblical times, city gates:

- Prevented enemies from entering the city through entry points in the city wall.
- Functioned as the center of city life—like a city hall or courthouse today. In various chambers inside the gatehouse, people paid their taxes, settled legal matters, and even met with the king. Soldiers were stationed there, too.
- Provided a gathering place for prophets, kings, priests, judges, and other city leaders. For example, Jehoshaphat (king of Judah) and Ahab (king of Israel) sat on their thrones in the gate of Samaria (1 Kings 22:10).

> **The Role of the Eastern Gate in the Life of the Messiah**
>
> The Bible predicts that the Messiah will enter the temple through the Eastern (or Beautiful) Gate. This prediction is taken so seriously by Islamic leaders that they have blocked the gate and built a cemetery in front of it in an effort to prevent the Messiah from entering the Temple Mount!
>
> Not only will the Messiah enter the temple through the Eastern Gate, tradition says that it will be the symbolic or literal location of the Last Judgment. Consider these Scriptures:
>
> - The Last Judgment will take place in the Jehoshaphat Valley, just east of Jerusalem (Joel 3:2, 12).
> - The power of God will establish Jerusalem as the Heavenly City (Zechariah 14:1–11).
> - After the Last Judgment, the saved will enter the gate of the Heavenly City (Isaiah 62:10; Revelation 21). Since the setting is on the east side of Jerusalem, the gate would be the Beautiful or Eastern Gate.

Topic D: Standing Stones

God's work in the past—the distant past or in our own past—is the foundation on which our belief in God and commitment to Him are built. Recognizing the importance of remembering what God had done for them, God's people in the Bible erected standing stones as memorials to God's supernatural acts on their behalf. The Canaanites also erected standing stones to their gods.

1. What is the difference between the standing stones mentioned in Genesis 28:18–22 and those described in 1 Kings 14:22–23?

2. Look up the following verses. What do they say about the pagan use of standing stones?

   a. Leviticus 26:1

   b. Deuteronomy 16:21–22 and Exodus 23:24

3. For each of the following passages, summarize the story or event and note the work of God that the standing stones commemorate or represent.

   a. Genesis 35:1–3, 14–15

   b. Exodus 24:1–5

   c. Joshua 3:14–17; 4:4–9

   d. Joshua 24:19–27

4. Read 1 Peter 2:4–12. In what ways is a believer like a living stone?

DATA FILE

At the high place at Gezer, ten stones (some more than twenty feet tall) stand in silent tribute to a now-forgotten event. Lonely sentinels on the ruins of ancient cities, these gigantic standing stones provide a glimpse into a custom popular thousands of years ago. Any travelers who saw the stones would know that something significant had happened there.

Long before the Israelites entered Canaan, pagans in the Middle East erected sacred stones to their gods, to declare covenants and treaties between cities or individuals, and to honor gods they believed caused an important event or provided a significant benefit.

The Hebrew word translated "standing stones" is *massebah* and means "to set up." Perhaps our practice of placing tombstones over the graves of loved ones is derived from a special standing stone called a *stele* (plural: *stelae*). These stones were erected as *masseboth* (standing stones) but had stories or inscriptions carved on them explaining their significance.

Archaeologists in the Middle East have unearthed many *stelae*, including one found in 1993 at Tel Dan that mentions the name "David"—the only extrabiblical reference to David ever discovered. To date, no *massebah* or *stele* specifically mentioned in the Bible has been found.

ғɑіth ʟesson

Time for Reflection

Read the following passage of Scripture and take the next few minutes to reflect on today's lesson and how it applies to your life.

> Goliath stood and shouted to the ranks of Israel, "Why do you come out and line up for battle? Am I not a Philistine, and are you not the servants of Saul? Choose a man and have him come down to me. If he is able to fight and kill me, we will become your subjects; but if I overcome him and kill him, you will become our subjects and serve us."
>
> Then the Philistine said, "This day I defy the ranks of Israel! Give me a man and let us fight each other."
>
> On hearing the Philistine's words, Saul and all the Israelites were dismayed and terrified. . . .
>
> David said to Saul, "Let no one lose heart on account of this Philistine; your servant will go and fight him. . . .
>
> "Your servant has killed both the lion and the bear; this uncircumcised Philistine will be like one of them, because he has defied the armies of the living God. The LORD who delivered me from the paw of the lion and the paw of the bear will deliver me from the hand of this Philistine."
>
> Saul said to David, "Go, and the LORD be with you." . . .
>
> David said to the Philistine, "You come against me with sword and spear and javelin, but I come against you in the name of the LORD Almighty, the God of the armies of Israel, whom you have defied. This day the LORD will hand you over to me, and I'll strike you down and cut off your head. Today I will give the carcasses of the Philistine army to the birds of the air and the beasts of the earth, and the whole world will know that there is a God in Israel. All those gathered here will know that it is not by sword or spear that the LORD saves; for the battle is the LORD's, and he will give all of you into our hands."
>
> 1 SAMUEL 17:8–11, 32, 36–37, 45–47

1. David clearly recognized that he stood at a crossroads and that he had a role to play in making the God of Israel known to the world. In what ways do you stand at a crossroads?

2. What could *you* do to publicly exert godly influence within your sphere of influence? In what arenas would God have you act to show that He is the Lord God?

3. How does God's call for you to exhibit Him in all that you do, think, and say affect what you do every day?

Action Points

Take a moment to review the key points you explored today. Then write down an action step (or steps) that you will commit to this week as a result of what you have learned.

1. *God wants His people to greatly influence the culture of their world.* That is why He placed His people in the land of Israel and wanted them to occupy the city of Gezer, which was an international crossroads.

   Likewise, God wants you and me—His followers today—to live at the crossroads of life. He wants us to live so publicly that we become a "flavoring influence" on our culture. Rather than isolating ourselves from the world, God wants us to actively participate in and control areas that shape our culture and the world as a whole.

   The crossroads at which I believe God wants me to make an impact is: _____

2. *Israel failed to conquer the Gezers of their world and as a
   result failed in their mission to be God's witnesses to the world.*

   We also fail in our mission as God's witnesses to the world
   when we don't take control and exert a godly influence on
   that which is significant in our culture.

   **What might be the consequences of your failure to be the
   witness God has called you to be? Be honest!**

3. *Just as the people of ancient Israel erected "standing stones"
   to commemorate God's supernatural actions on their behalf
   (such as when He gave them the Ten Commandments), God
   wants each of us to be a* massebah—*a living, standing stone.*

   In 1 Peter 2:4–5, we learn that we "like living stones are
   being built into a spiritual house." Each of us is like a piece
   of stone that God is shaping and cutting in order to build
   His kingdom. He wants us to exhibit Him to a watching
   world. As we live godly lives, non-Christians will see our
   good deeds and be drawn toward God—just as the people
   in ancient times were reminded about what God had done
   for them when they saw standing stones.

   **What kind of standing stone are you? What about your
   life says to other people, "The Lord is God"?**

   **What specific action(s) could you take today to become
   a standing stone to other people in the future? Pray that
   God will empower you in that decision and watch as God
   becomes known to other people through you.**

wet feet

questions to think about

1. What are some of the barriers we allow to exist between us and the calling God has given us to fulfill? In other words, what keeps us from completely trusting Him and committing our lives to Him?

2. How does who we believe God to be influence how much we trust Him in daily life?

video notes

The Jordan River

Stepping into the Jordan

The Meaning of Jesus' Baptism

video Highlights

Look at the map of geographical features of the land of Israel on page 30. Note the coastal plain, the Shephelah, and the Central Mountains, with which we became familiar during the first session. In this session, our attention is drawn to the Great Rift Valley, particularly the Jordan River, which runs down the valley from the foot of Mount Hermon through the Sea of Galilee and into the Dead Sea. The children of Israel approached the Promised Land from the wilderness to the east, choosing to cross the Jordan River near Jericho, just north of the Dead Sea.

1. From the stories we've read in the Bible, most of us have an image of what the Jordan River looks like. What about the river surprised you when you saw it in the video?

2. What did God demonstrate when He miraculously guided the Israelites across the Jordan River—and to whom?

3. What similarities do you see between Jesus' baptism in the Jordan River and the Israelites' crossing of the Jordan in order to possess the Promised Land?

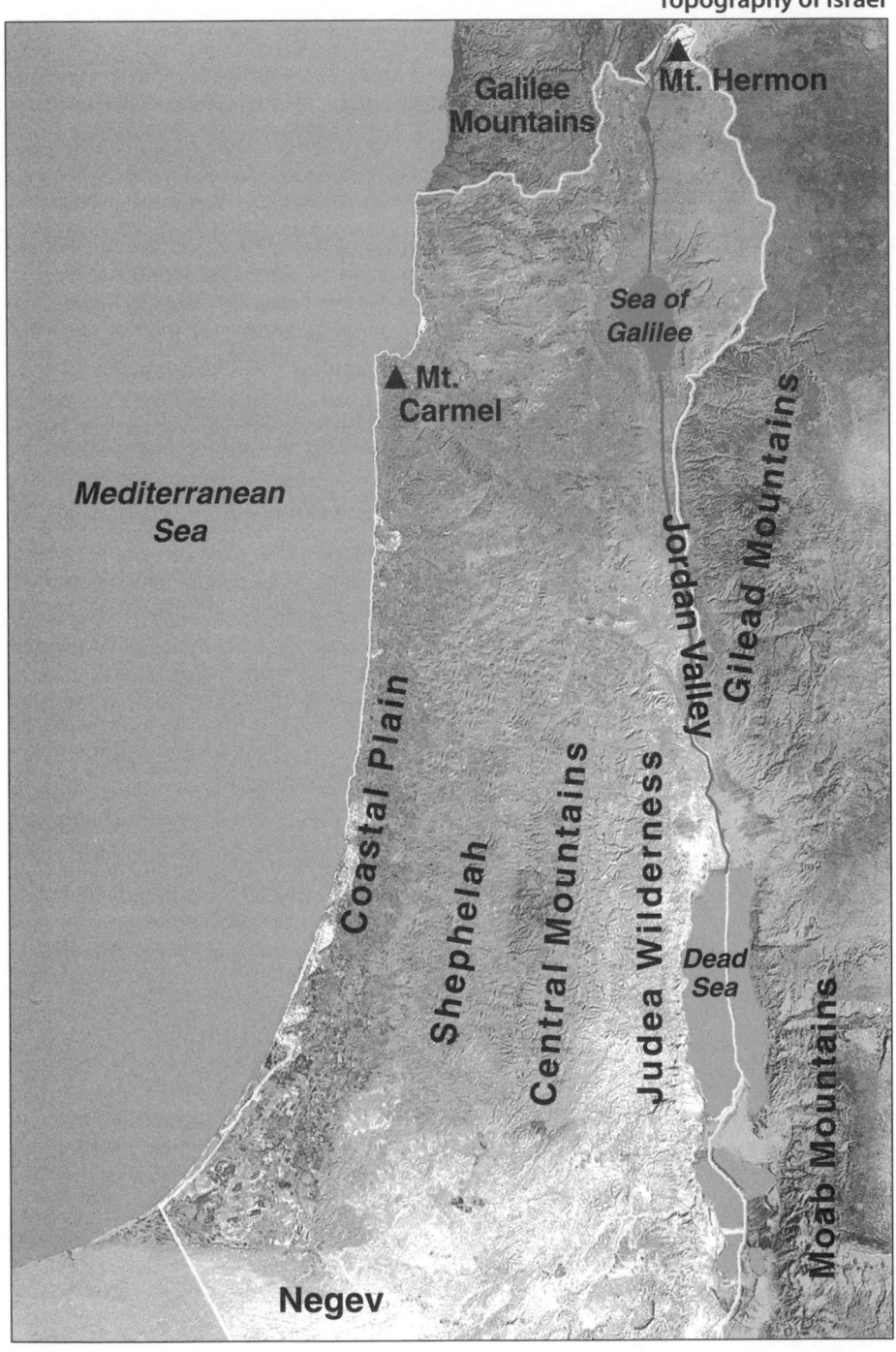

Topography of Israel

Galilee Mountains

Mt. Hermon

Mt. Carmel

Sea of Galilee

Gilead Mountains

Mediterranean Sea

Jordan Valley

Coastal Plain

Shephelah

Central Mountains

Judea Wilderness

Dead Sea

Moab Mountains

Negev

small group Bible Discovery

Topic A: Crossing the Jordan River

1. Each of the following Bible passages tells a story involving the Jordan River. Review each story and note the significant details that stand out to you.

   a. Deuteronomy 1:21–32; 3:23–28; 34:1–4

   b. 1 Kings 16:29–33; 17:1–6

   c. 2 Samuel 17:15–22

   d. 2 Kings 2:1–2, 5–15

2. What common threads do you see in these stories?

DATA FILE

The Jordan River
- Starts in northern Israel at the foot of Mount Hermon, more than 1,500 feet above sea level, and ends almost 1,400 feet below sea level at the Dead Sea.
- Meanders for 200 miles from Mount Hermon to the Dead Sea, a distance of 90 miles as the crow flies.
- Flows through the Great Rift Valley, a cut in the earth's crust that extends all the way to Lake Victoria in southern Africa.
- Is one of the fastest-flowing rivers for its size in the world.
- Is today dammed up where it runs out of the Sea of Galilee to help meet the State of Israel's water needs.

Topic B: Commitment Means Making the First Move

Many Christians today are reluctant to step out in faith to pursue the calling God has given to them. As you read the following Scripture passages, take note of what making a commitment to follow God's calling required.

1. Read Joshua 3:5–17. Who was required to take action when the Israelites crossed the Jordan River? What was the result?

2. In faith, what did Joshua tell the people? (See Joshua 3:5.)

3. What did God reveal to Joshua? (See Joshua 3:7–8.)

4. What were some of God's reasons for enabling the Israelites to cross the Jordan River? (See Joshua 3:10.)

The Ark of the Covenant

5. Clearly God could have divided the Jordan River at any time He chose. Why do you think He waited until the priests entered the water carrying the ark?

6. Write out your own "wet feet" concept—what it really means for you to follow God and pursue His calling.

Topic C: The Ark of God

The ark of the covenant became the focal point of God's presence among His people. It was so important to God that He described its construction before describing any other sacred object—even before the tabernacle (Exodus 25:10–22).

1. What was the ark of the covenant's central purpose? (See Exodus 25:16.) What other purpose did it serve? (See Exodus 25:22.)

2. On the Day of Atonement (Yom Kippur), the great holy day of the Bible, what would happen? (See Leviticus 16:2.)

3. What did the ark of the covenant symbolize to the people? (See Psalm 91:4; 99:1.)

4. During the siege of Jericho, where was the ark of the covenant carried? What did this symbolize? (See Joshua 6:1–11.)

DATA FILE

The Ark of the Covenant:
- Was made of acacia wood, an extremely hard wood common to the Sinai Peninsula.
- Was three feet nine inches long, two feet three inches wide, and two feet three inches tall.
- Was gold plated and had a gold rim around the top.
- Stood on four legs, and on each side were two gold rings in which poles were inserted so the Levites (the priestly tribe) could carry it.
- Had a cover—called the mercy seat or atonement seat—that was made of pure gold. On top of the lid were two cherubim—probably sphinxes—whose wings stretched over the cover.
- Was viewed by the Israelites as God's footstool (1 Chronicles 28:2).

5. Years later, even the priests of Israel became unfaithful and dishonored God (1 Samuel 2:27–36), so God ceased to honor His people and removed His strength from them. Read 1 Samuel 4:1–11, and list the consequences that followed. What did the Israelites depend on to save them? Why do you think their efforts failed?

6. According to 1 Corinthians 3:16–17, where does God choose to reveal Himself today?

DID YOU KNOW?

Following Middle Eastern custom, God instructed Moses to make two summary documents of the covenant He made with His people. These documents (each of which contained all Ten Commandments) were His guarantee that His Word would never fail. Normally, each covenanting party took a summary copy of the covenant and placed it in their most sacred place, where it would be read regularly as a reminder of the covenant.

Apparently God gave both copies to Moses, ordering him to place them into the ark. Imagine Moses' reaction when he learned that the most sacred place for God and for Israel was the same—the ark of the covenant!

Topic D: Up, Out of the Jordan: The Baptism of Jesus

The greatest New Testament event to take place in relationship to the Jordan River was the baptism of Jesus.

1. Consider the parallels between the symbolism of Jesus' baptism and the creation story:

The Water	Genesis 1:2	
	Matthew 3:16	
The Spirit	Genesis 1:2	
	Matthew 3:16	
God's Approval	Genesis 1:31	
	Matthew 3:17	
A New Creation	Genesis 1:3–30	
	Matthew 11:2–6	
Temptation	Genesis 3:1–7	
	Matthew 4:1–11	

2. Why do you think Jesus said that His followers would be "greater" than John the Baptist? (See Luke 7:28.)

3. In John 14:9–13, Jesus answers a question and in so doing explains His calling. What was His calling? How does it compare to the calling of the Israelites as they went in to possess the Promised Land?

ꜰɑith Lesson

Time for Reflection

Read the following passage of Scripture silently and take the next few minutes to consider the obstacles that stand between you and God's calling on your life.

> Joshua said to the Israelites, "Come here and listen to the words of the LORD your God. This is how you will know that the living God is among you and that he will certainly drive out before you the Canaanites, Hittites, Hivites, Perizzites, Girgashites, Amorites and Jebusites. See, the ark of the covenant of the Lord of all the earth will go into the Jordan ahead of you. Now then, choose twelve men from the tribes of Israel, one from each tribe. And as soon as the priests who carry the ark of the LORD—the Lord of all the earth— set foot in the Jordan, its waters flowing downstream will be cut off and stand up in a heap."
>
> So when the people broke camp to cross the Jordan, the priests carrying the ark of the covenant went ahead of them. Now the Jordan is at flood stage all during harvest. Yet as soon as the priests who carried the ark reached the Jordan and their feet touched the water's edge, the water from upstream stopped flowing. It piled up in a heap a great distance away, at a town called Adam in the vicinity of Zarethan, while the water flowing down to the Sea of the Arabah (the Salt Sea) was completely cut off. So the people crossed over opposite Jericho. The priests who carried the ark of the covenant of the LORD stood firm on dry ground in the middle of the Jordan, while all Israel passed by until the whole nation had completed the crossing on dry ground.
>
> JOSHUA 3:9–17

1. Take a moment to imagine what it was like for the Israelites to stand on the banks of the Jordan River on that glorious day. Imagine their excitement—a new homeland. Imagine their fear—they didn't know what awaited them. Imagine their

anticipation—what would God do? His ark was headed into floodwaters! Imagine their awe—to walk across the Jordan River on dry land.

2. Imagine that you are standing on the banks of the Jordan River and the land on the other side represents your life's mission or a specific task God has given you. What represents the "Jordan River," the barrier in your life that keeps you from entering into the life God intends for you? How might you take a step of faith to cross over that "Jordan River" in your life?

3. Think of a time in your life, or in the life of someone you know, where a total commitment to God brought about a great display of His power and blessing. How can that testimony of God's love and faithfulness be a "standing stone" for you that will encourage you to pursue God's calling for your life?

Action Points

Take a moment to review the key points you explored today. Then, determine the step (or steps) of commitment that you will take this week to carry out God's calling in your life.

1. *The Israelites viewed the Jordan River as a barrier between them and the Promised Land where God had called them to live.* As Christians, we also face issues and obstacles that stand between us and the work to which God has called us.

   Think about your life. What is the barrier that keeps you from making a total commitment to God?

What about that barrier is so frightening to you that you fail to put your complete trust in God? Do you truly believe that barrier is beyond God's influence?

2. *When the Israelites reached the banks of the Jordan River, they had to choose whether or not they would be totally committed to God.* They had to choose whether anything was outside of God's control and influence—including the barrier of raging water. They had to decide whether they would put their faith in the God who had led them through the desert or put their faith in the Canaanites' fertility gods who supposedly controlled water.

Likewise, Christians today must be willing to be totally committed to God. We must not allow anything to stand between us and the calling God has placed before us. We must step out in faith in order for His power to be released in our lives.

The priests took a step of faith into the flooded Jordan River and saw God do a miracle. What step of faith can you, your family, and/or your church take so that God's power can be more visible in your community? How, in other words, might you "get your feet wet"?

3. *Jesus' baptism in the Jordan River symbolized God's creation of a new order—a new, loving, caring way of doing things that the Spirit of God was bringing to the world.* As followers of Jesus, we are God's ambassadors who are called to bring the healing, love, and comfort of God into the lives of broken people.

   What are the issues, concerns, problems, or aspects of your community in which God would have you serve as His ambassador? In what way might you bring Christ's restoring, healing love to a hurting individual in your community? What step of faith could you take this week to actively rely on His power?

FAITH PROFILE

Deceived by Appearances

The Great Rift Valley, through which the Jordan River flows, is arid and has poor soil that absorbs little water and will not sustain vegetation. Along the river, however, the soil is suitable for vegetation, and dense plants grow. This lush growth, which the Bible refers to as the "thickets of the Jordan" (Jeremiah 49:19; Zechariah 11:3), does not extend far from the water's edge.

A spring probably created the lush oasis that Lot saw as he surveyed the land from the edge of the Judea Wilderness near Bethel (Genesis 13:10–13). He "looked up and saw that the whole plain of the Jordan was well watered." As we know from Scripture, however, the most obvious choice isn't always the best one—or the one that pleases the Lord.

When Lot left Abraham, he not only left the wilderness, where a person had to depend on God for survival, but chose to leave Abraham's God. That, in turn, spelled disaster for Lot and his family. In his greed, Lot had chosen what appeared to be the best land, but the watered portion of the riverbed was too small and dense for his flocks, and the plains along the river lacked the vegetation necessary to sustain life. So Lot's solution was to move to the well-watered, pagan city of Sodom where he became a leader among idolatrous people who worshiped the Canaanite fertility gods and practiced all forms of sexual perversion. He "sat in the gate" of Sodom in a position of honor, and only God's mercy and the loyalty of his uncle Abraham allowed him and his daughters to escape God's judgment.

After losing everything else dear to him, including his wife, Lot discovered that even his daughters had become like the people of Sodom (Genesis 19:30–38). His grandchildren became the people of Moab and Ammon, infamous in the Bible for their idolatry and evil ways.

Lot's profile serves as a reminder to us. Our culture may appear to be desirable and healthful, making it easy for us to become caught up in secular society's values and practices. The only way to be free of today's "Sodoms," however, is to make choices according to God's standards. Abraham knew this lesson well.

first fruits

questions to think about

1. How might you have felt if you were one of the Israelites who had crossed the Jordan River into the Promised Land and had immediately encountered the fortified city of Jericho?

2. What are some of the intimidating, well-established, evil aspects of our society that Christians must confront if they follow God's calling and seek to bring His standards to bear on society?

   Lack of Morality
   No Guilt

   Bill – Defeating Darwinism by Opening Minds

3. Consider what is required to stand up and battle against the established evils of our society. In what ways are your feelings similar to or unlike what you imagine you would have felt as an Israelite facing Jericho?

video notes

The City of Jericho *lowest, oldest, 7,000 BC Tower*

Abraham Came Town was 7000 yrs old
Cross roads, lush, water

Rahab - *2 spys - need this road -*
when we heard you were coming we
were afraid = your God is God of Heaven
& of earth

angel - Messenger of God,
God's Battle Strategy *Commander of the Lord's army*
Tells Gods: -
Cursed before the Lord is any man who
rebuilds Jericho Harm to children
God wants us to give him 1st fruits of
ourselves -

First Fruits *when God gives -*
a way of saying this is all I have
but to show you I trust you & that
will give me the rest I'm bringing it

Kings, Hiel took the city
rebuilt it lost sons
we have been gifted to be used by God
not want same for myself -

video highlights

Locate Jericho on the map of Israel below.

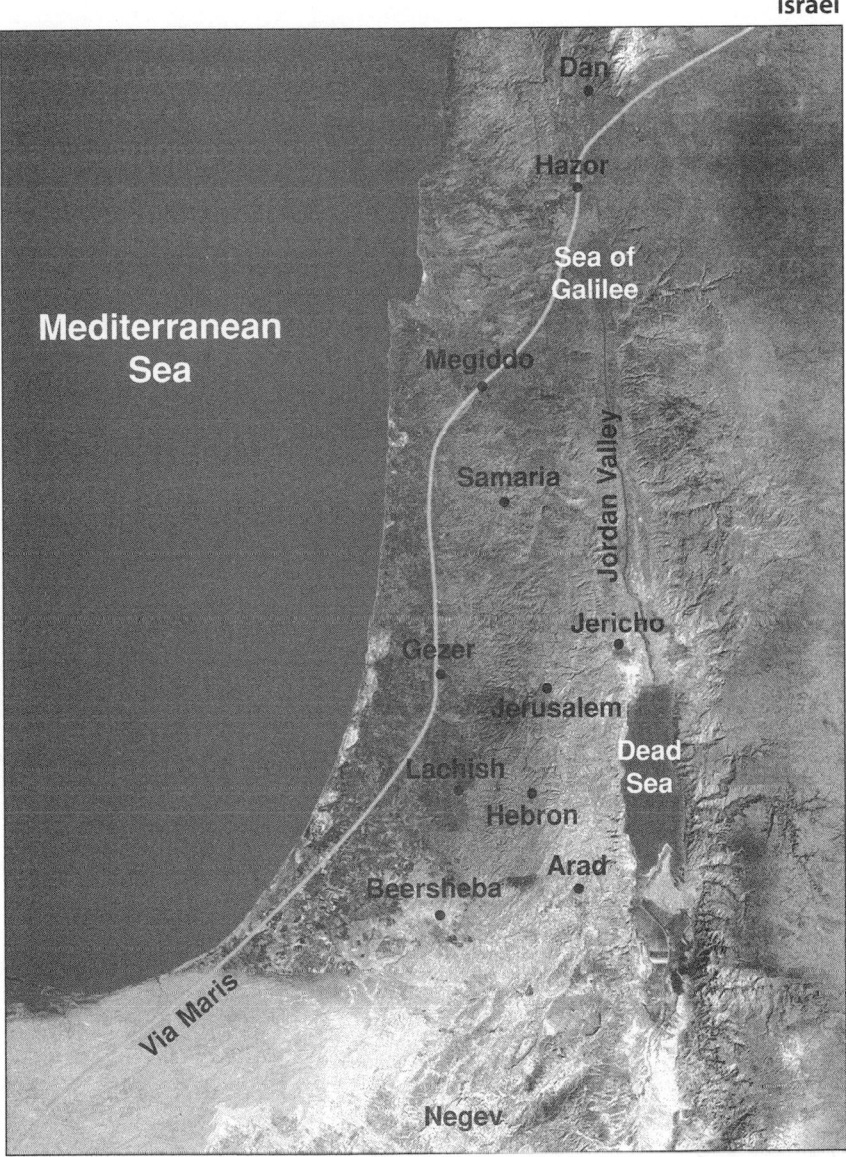

1. Why was Jericho such a strategic city during ancient times? *location to cross between the two highways*

2. Were you surprised to learn that Rahab is listed in the genealogy of Jesus? Why or why not?
   Rahab was mother-in-law of Ruth as Boaz was her son

3. In what ways did God clearly communicate that the battle for Jericho was His? *They were afraid because they had heard of God's power*

4. How has your view of God's principle of "first fruits" changed as a result of seeing this video?
   I never really knew, your life is your first fruits

at home

small group bible discovery

Topic A: Rahab—A Woman with an Incredible Story

1. What happened when Joshua sent two spies into Jericho? (See Joshua 2:1–7.)

2. What did Rahab say to the foreign spies? (See Joshua 2:8–13.) Why did she risk so much to protect them?

3. What did the spies promise to do for her? (See Joshua 2:14, 17–19.)

4. Why do you think God allowed the Israelites to spare the lives of Rahab and her family when Jericho was destroyed? (See Joshua 6:20–25.)

5. What do you understand about the character of God when you read Matthew 1:1–7 and discover Rahab's name in the genealogy of Jesus?

Topic B: The People God Can Use

1. Look up each of the following passages and summarize what you discover about the people God has used to carry out His plans.

   a. Genesis 38:6–7, 11–19; Matthew 1:3a

   b. Joshua 2:1–15; 6:22–25; Matthew 1:5a

   c. Ruth 1:1–8, 14–16, 22; Matthew 1:5b

   d. 2 Samuel 11:1–5, 14–17; Matthew 1:6

2. In light of their life stories, what is the significance of God choosing Rahab, Bathsheba, Tamar, and Ruth to be in Jesus' ancestral line?

3. With these biblical accounts in mind, who else can you think of who came from a sinful past, chose a personal relationship with God through Jesus, and went on to become a powerful instrument in sharing the message of Jesus?

Topic C: God's Love of Holiness

The conquest of Canaan and the destruction of cities such as Jericho poses an ethical dilemma for many Bible readers. How could the God of love and mercy demand such merciless destruction of the inhabitants of the Promised Land? Although none of us can completely understand the sovereign God of the universe, the Bible reveals much about how seriously God views sin.

1. What kind of a world did God create from the chaos of water? (See Genesis 1–2, especially 1:2, 31.)

2. How did Adam and Eve—the crown of God's creation—respond toward God in the Garden of Eden? (See Genesis 3:1–12.)

3. What has God always wanted His people to be? (See Joshua 24:19–23; Leviticus 11:44; 1 Peter 1:15; 2:9.)

4. What do each of the following passages reveal about how God views sin?

Numbers 15:32–40	
Exodus 19:5–6	
Exodus 32:1, 7–14, 31–35	
1 Corinthians 6:18–20	

5. In contrast to the Israelites, who were called to be holy before God, what were the pagan inhabitants of Canaan like? (See Leviticus 18:1–5, 24–30; Deuteronomy 18:9–13.)

Topic D: When God's Judgment Falls

1. As the Israelites prepared to battle the pagan nations in the Promised Land, what instructions did God give them concerning their attacks on cities such as Jericho, and why? (See Deuteronomy 20:16–18; Joshua 6:16–18, 21–24.)

DATA FILE

The Judgment of God

The judgment of God (called *cherem* in Hebrew) is translated "totally devoted to God" or "utterly destroyed." In modern English, we might say "damned." Only such total judgment could remove the pollution of sin so that God's creation would again honor Him.

The Bible provides several examples of God's *cherem* falling on sinful people:

- Genesis 6–8—God flooded the whole earth to wash away a perverse human race.
- Genesis 19—God poured fire and brimstone on the evil cities of Sodom and Gomorrah.
- Numbers 16—Because they defied Him, God destroyed Korah, Dathan, Abiram, and their followers, as well as all of their family members and belongings.

The conquest of Canaan was another step in God's plan to reclaim His world. Only the total destruction of the sinful Canaanites would make the land fit for God's people to serve Him and enable them to become a blessing to all nations so that the world would know that Yahweh is God. To bring about His judgment and restoration, God chose as His instruments the same creatures who had sinned against Him.

2. What accompanied the Israelites as they marched around Jericho? Why? (See Joshua 6:6–9.)

3. What similarities do you note between Joshua 6:15–16, 20 and 1 Thessalonians 4:16?

4. Look up the following verses and describe God's response to and judgment of sin.

Genesis 6:5–9, 13–14, 17–18; 7:23	
Genesis 18:20–33; 19:1, 12–13, 24–25	
Numbers 16:1–11, 20–35	
Numbers 25:1–9	
Revelation 20:7–10	

5. Contrast God's judgment of sin with what we read in John 3:16 and 1 John 1:9.

DATA FILE

The Holy, the Common, and the Abominable

The Old Testament view of sin and judgment produced a concept of reality divided into three parts: the holy, the common, and the abominable (unclean).

The Holy

Anything devoted to Yahweh or used in His service was considered holy. God made some things, such as the Sabbath, holy. Some things became holy (such as first fruits) because they were offered to God in service. Once something had been given to God, it was His alone.

The worst kind of sin was to use something holy for one's personal benefit. Jericho had been given to God, so it was not to be inhabited again. Israel, as a nation, had been set apart to serve God, so it could not worship anyone or anything else. And according to the New Testament, every Christian is holy, set apart to serve God. So we cannot and must not serve any other person, idea, or thing. Every part of our lives should be dedicated to serving the Lord—including our occupations, families, and recreation. Nothing is to be done for our benefit alone. To do so is to place ourselves under His judgment.

The Common

In the Old Testament, things that belonged to the people were considered common: household possessions, animals, land, etc. These things were to be used in godly ways, but they were under the stewardship of the people who owned them. In the New Testament, however, the holy and common were joined. Everything, even mundane things, is now to be used in God's service.

The prophet Zechariah said that when the Messiah returns, even the bowls used in family cooking will be as sacred as those used in temple worship. "And on that day there will no longer be a Canaanite in the house of the Lord Almighty" (Zechariah 14:20–21). That is the story of Jericho. The Canaanites living there had polluted God's land and had to be removed by His judgment. Then the holy people of God could begin to find ways to serve Him in every part of their lives.

(continued on page 54)

(continued from page 53)

The Abominable

God detests abominations—anything associated with the worship of other gods and any behavior that perverts the lifestyle God intended human beings to live. Leviticus 18 contains a list of unlawful behaviors (e.g., incest, adultery, homosexuality, bestiality). As He demonstrated by sending the Great Flood, the judgment on Sodom and Gomorrah, and various judgments on the Israelites, God will judge people who practice these behaviors.

Topic E: Set Apart for God

The principle of "first fruits" reinforces the truth that God is the giver of everything. To give God the first fruits is an act of faith that expresses trust in God to provide the rest. To take the first fruits for ourselves is to deny God's ownership of our blessings and to fail to live by faith.

1. What was God's desire concerning the first portion of whatever blessings He gave to Israel? (Read Leviticus 23:9–14.)

2. How did this principle apply to the spoils of Jericho, the first city that God gave to Israel? (Read Joshua 6:19, 26.)

3. Instead of obeying God and giving Him the first fruits of the Canaanites' wealth, what did one of the Israelites do? What happened as a consequence? (See Joshua 7:1–12, 24–26.)

WHAT IS A *MEZUZAH?*

Attached to the doorpost of every religious Jewish home is a small container called a *mezuzah* that holds a rolled parchment inscribed with Bible verses (the text of Deuteronomy 4:4–9; 11:13–21). A Jewish person entering the home touches the *mezuzah* and then kisses his or her fingers as an expression of devotion to the verses it contains. The Jews also customarily say, "May God protect my going out and coming in, now and forever."

The Tradition Behind It

Jewish scholars base the custom of the *mezuzah* on Deuteronomy 6:6, 9: "These commandments that I give you today are to be upon your hearts. . . . Write them on the doorframes of your houses and on your gates." The physical presence of a copy of the Deuteronomy commandments provided an excellent reminder of God's desires for His people.

Jericho's Ruins Were Like a Mezuzah

The main, eastern gate or doorway to the Promised Land is the mountain pass guarded by Jericho. Appropriately, God commanded that the city's ruins be left as a testimony, like a *mezuzah,* that the land belonged to Him and that His people who lived in it sought to serve Him. God wanted His mark of ownership to remain on the land as a reminder that its inhabitants must live by His laws.

4. As the Israelites watched God's judgment focusing on the tribes, then the clans of Judah, and finally on Achan's family itself (Joshua 7:13–18), what effect do you think that process had on the people? What did God's punishment (Joshua 7:24–25) communicate about God's tolerance of sin?

5. When you read about what happened to Hiel of Bethel, are you surprised? Why or why not? (See Joshua 6:26–27 and 1 Kings 16:29–34.)

6. What were the ruins of Jericho to communicate to all future generations? (See Joshua 6:20–21, 24.)

ғaith Lesson

Time for Reflection

Read the following passage of Scripture silently and take the next few minutes to consider how God uses people who are committed to Him to accomplish His purposes.

Now Jericho was tightly shut up because of the Israelites. No one went out and no one came in.

Then the LORD said to Joshua, "See, I have delivered Jericho into your hands, along with its king and its fighting men. March around the city once with all the armed men. Do this for six days. Have seven priests carry trumpets of rams' horns in front of the ark. On the seventh day, march around the city seven times, with the priests blowing the trumpets. When you hear them sound a long blast on the trumpets, have all the people give a loud shout; then the wall of the city will collapse and the people will go up, every man straight in."

. . . On the seventh day, they got up at daybreak and marched around the city seven times in the same manner, except that on that day they circled the city seven times. The seventh time around, when the priests sounded the trumpet blast, Joshua commanded the people, "Shout! For the LORD has given you the city! The city and all that is in it are to be devoted to the LORD. Only Rahab the prostitute and all who are with her in her house shall be spared, because she hid the spies we sent. But keep away from the devoted things, so that you will not bring about your own destruction by taking any of them. Otherwise you will make the camp of Israel liable to destruction and bring trouble on it. All the silver and gold and the articles of bronze and iron are sacred to the LORD and must go into his treasury."

When the trumpets sounded, the people shouted, and at the sound of the trumpet, when the people gave a loud shout, the wall collapsed; so every man charged straight in, and they took the city.

They devoted the city to the LORD and destroyed with the sword every living thing in it—men and women, young and old, cattle, sheep and donkeys.

JOSHUA 6:1–5, 15–21

1. When the Israelites marched around Jericho, the ark of the covenant went with them. Why is it important to remember that God is with you as you seek to live by His truths and reveal Him to a culture that rejects Him?

2. What is encouraging to you about the fact that God used sinful people in spite of their pasts and even chose them to be in the lineage of the Messiah?

3. If you are a follower of Jesus, you are holy and "set apart" for God. What does the fact that you are holy tell you about the lifestyle you should lead? What changes do you need to make in order to live out your calling?

Action Points

After you have reviewed the key points of this lesson, take a moment to jot down an action step (or steps) that you will commit to this week as a result of what you have learned today.

1. *As the Israelites took possession of the Promised Land, God clearly demonstrated that the battle against its pagan inhabitants was His battle, not theirs.*

   Likewise, as we seek to bring God's value system into our culture and to confront that which is contrary to God's way, we need to remember that the battle is the Lord's. He is the one who seeks to reclaim the world He created, and we are His instruments in that process.

   As you confront the secular world's value system, which battles will you face?

   In what ways can you let them be God's battles, not yours?

2. *God's people are to follow the Old Testament principle of "first fruits," meaning we are to offer God the first part of what we receive as our provision.* By doing so, we acknowledge that God is the source of our provision and that we trust Him to continue to provide for us.

   If we give ourselves to God as His holy, "set-apart" people, He will take care of the rest! But if we use what has been set apart for God's use to benefit ourselves, we break the first-fruits principle. God does not provide for us so that we can honor ourselves. God gives us what we have—

money, time, talents, etc.—so that He can use us as agents in His service.

When you give God the first portion of the blessings He gives you, what are you demonstrating—to yourself and to a watching world?

What has God provided for you to use in His service? In what ways might you be taking back God's first fruits in regard to your talents, your financial resources, your occupation, etc.?

confronting evil

questions to think about

1. When you hear the word "Philistine," which images come to mind?

2. Even though God clearly tells His people that the values and lifestyle of the world's culture—whether it is the world of the Israelites or our world today—are sinful, we still find ourselves being drawn to them. Why is that?

3. What can happen when we seek to follow God in most areas of our lives but have a few areas that are not committed to Him?

4. What is the result of compromising with a world that doesn't live according to God's values?

video notes

The Philistines—the People, the Land

The Importance of Fulfilling God's Calling

Samson—His Calling, His Failing

The Consequences of Compromise

video Highlights

1. Look at the map of Israel on page 64. Note the location of the Via Maris and the valleys that extend from the coastal plain into the Shephelah and the mountains. How does this help you to understand the important role this area played in the lives of the Israelites?

2. What did you learn about the Philistines and their culture that you did not know before watching this video? How does this help you to understand the significance of what took place between the Israelites and the Philistines?

3. What happened to Samson that caused him to fail to live up to his calling?

4. Eli sent the ark of the covenant into battle, hoping that God would then rescue the Israelites. Why do you think Eli's strategy didn't work? What message does this story have for Christians today?

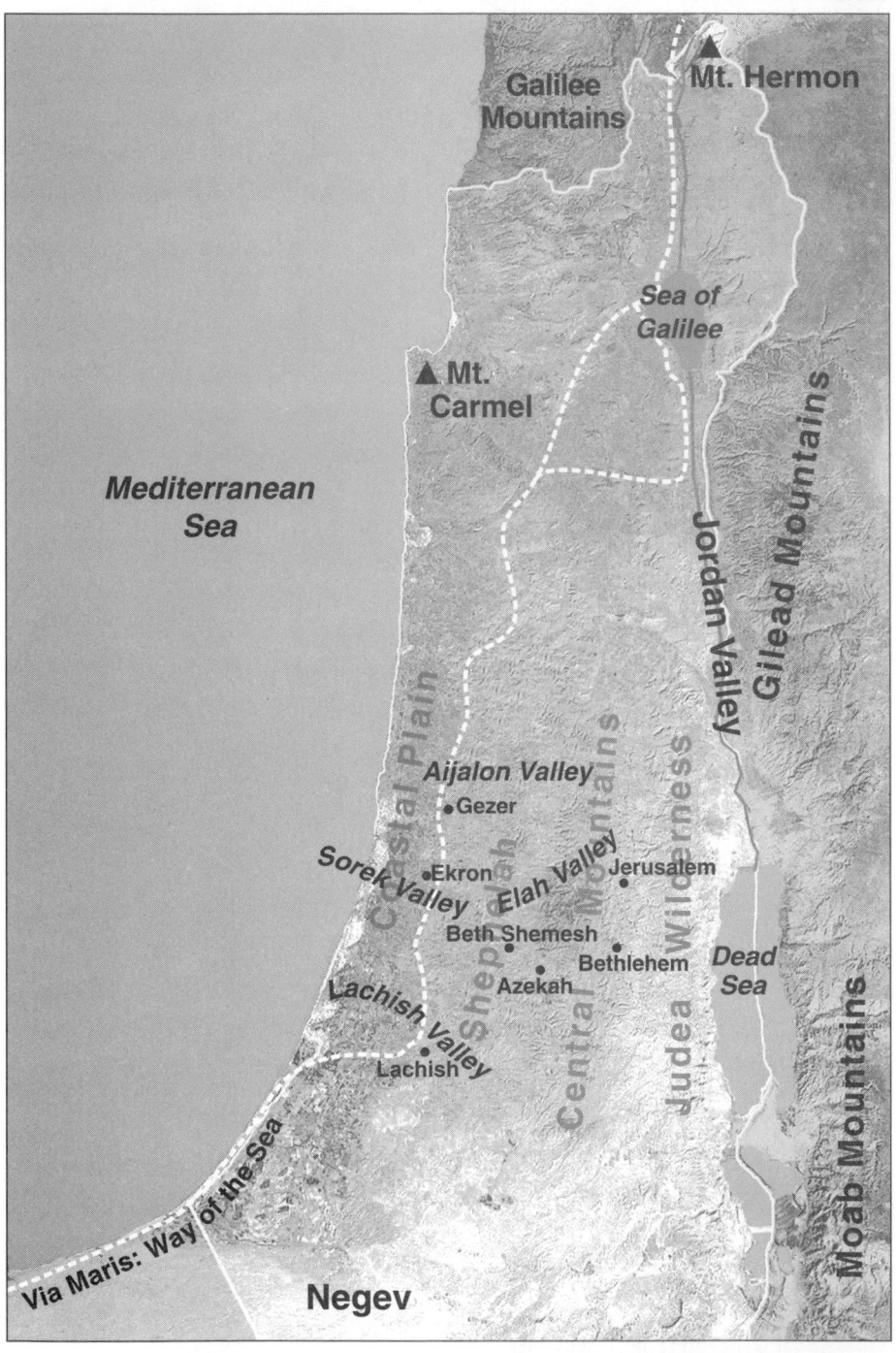

Israel

SPOTLIGHT ON THE EVIDENCE

The Making of a Tel

Israel is dotted with distinctive hills called *tels* that are characterized by steep sides and flat tops. (*Tel*, incidentally, is the Hebrew spelling, which we use in this study. The English spelling is *tell*.) These hills comprise layers and layers of ancient settlements, each of which was built on the ruins of a previous settlement. In general terms, here's how tels, including Tel Beth Shemesh, were formed.

Stage 1: People settled on the site, eventually building a wall and gate. Often a rampart was built against the wall to protect the hill from erosion and to keep enemies away from the base of the wall.

Stage 2: The settlement was abandoned, due to war, drought, etc. Then the ruins faded into the landscape.

Stage 3: People moved back to the same spot, filled in holes, gathered larger building stones, leveled off the hill, and rebuilt. Then the city's success attracted enemies . . . and the cycle of destruction and rebuilding continued.

(continued on page 66)

Diagram of a Tel

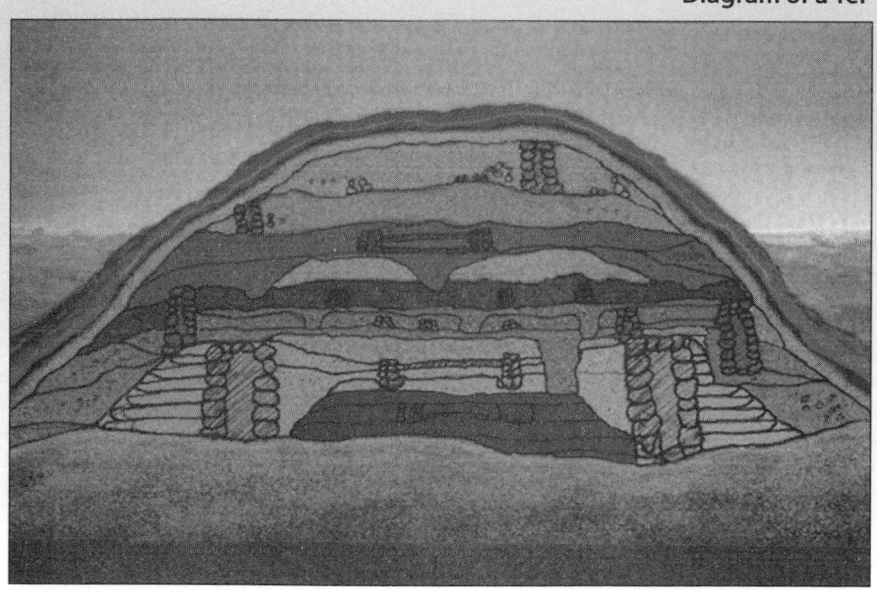

(continued from page 65)

Stage 4: Layers upon layers of ruins accumulated (sort of like a layer cake), so the hill became higher. Each layer—or stratum—records what life was like during a particular time. Artifacts discovered in the tel reveal a great deal about how people lived during specific time periods.

Tels help us understand more clearly the Bible's message by providing relevant information about life in biblical times. Each tel is, in effect, a unique gift from God to help us better understand His Word.

The Making of a City

The environment of the Middle East, including Israel, is harsh and mostly unsuitable for settlement. For a location such as Beth Shemesh to be habitable, three conditions were needed:

Fresh Water

Although rainfall is plentiful in some regions of Israel, most rain falls during the winter. Many ancient communities stored rainwater in cisterns. If a season received below-average rainfall, cisterns dried up and people abandoned their city. If an enemy laid siege to a city, only the cisterns inside the city walls were available, and often the water ran out and the city fell. Jerusalem was built next to the spring of Gihon. Meggido, Hazor, and Gezer had tunnels dug through bedrock in order to reach fresh water.

Profitable Occupation

People needed the opportunity to either grow a consistent food supply or to be able to buy food.

- Olive trees flourished in Judea and Galilee.
- Wheat grew in the valleys of Judea and Jezreel.
- Shepherds raised sheep and goats in the wilderness.
- Chorazin and Ekron had large, olive-oil processing facilities.
- Jerusalem was famous for its purple dye.
- Some cities supplied travelers on the Via Maris, the major trade route.

A Defensible Location

The political climate in the ancient Middle East was volatile, so cities were typically built on hills ringing fertile valleys so inhabitants could defend themselves.

Why Beth Shemesh?
- Guarded a passage between the coastal plain (Philistine territory) and the mountains of Judah (Israelite territory).
- Was founded during the early Bronze Age—nearly 5,000 years ago.
- Was destroyed and rebuilt at least six times, once by the Babylonians on their way to destroy Jerusalem for the first time (588–587 B.C.).
- Contained many olive oil and fabric dying installations and wheat production industries during King David's time.

small group bible discovery

Topic A: The Shephelah

The foothills—the Shephelah—served as a buffer zone between the Philistine territory of the coastal plain and the mountains where the Israelites lived. Because control of the Shephelah ensured the security and power of the dominant culture, many battles between the Philistines and the Israelites took place there. To establish the dominance of His values and to preserve His plan for the salvation of the world, God raised up heroes to confront the Philistines in the Shephelah.

1. Investigate the following events that took place in the Shephelah. Note where these events took place, who God raised up to battle the Philistines, and the result.

    a. 1 Samuel 13:5–7; 14:1–16, 22–23, 31

    b. 1 Samuel 17:1–9, 16, 32, 48–52

    c. Judges 13:1–5, 24–25; 15:3–5, 14–17

> ## DATA FILE
>
> **The Shephelah**
> - a twelve- to fifteen-mile-wide region of foothills in Judea that are located between the coastal plain to the west and the Judea Mountains to the east.
> - The valleys of the Shephelah functioned as corridors between the mountains and the coastal plain.
> - Served as a place of contact—peaceful or not—where the Israelites interacted with the Philistines. Most Philistine-Israelite conflicts took place here.
> - Symbolizes for us the places where God's values meet the pagan practices of Western culture. Like the Israelites, we have a choice: to withdraw to the "mountains" or to be on the front line, confront the secular values of our world, and with God's blessing seek to gain control of the "coastal plain" in our neighborhoods, cities, country, and the world.

Topic B: The Philistines

1. What do the following passages reveal about the Philistines and their culture?

    a. 1 Samuel 13:16–22

    b. 1 Samuel 31:1–13

    c. 1 Kings 22:51–53; 2 Kings 1:1–3; Matthew 12:24–28

    d. Judges 1:19; 2:1–3

DATA FILE

The Philistines

History

Sailed from the Aegean world (Greece) and settled along the coast of Palestine about 1100 B.C., about the time the Israelites entered the Promised Land from the east. Developed a sophisticated culture in various city states.

Location

The five main Philistine cities were located near the Via Maris trade route, which went through the coastal plain. So, the Philistines dominated world trade and greatly influenced other nations.

Industry

Had an elaborate olive pressing industry. (At Ekron alone, about 200 installations produced olive oil—perhaps more than 1,000 tons!) Also famous for iron making.

Military Might

Philistine soldiers were quite tall, clean shaven, and wore breastplates and small kilts. The soldiers carried small shields and fought with straight swords and spears.

Artistic Skill

Created intricate pottery with red and black geometric designs on white backgrounds.

Religion

Very sophisticated and immoral. The people built carefully planned temples in Gaza, Ashdod, and Beth Shean. Dagon, their main god, was thought to be the god of grain. Believed to be his mistress, the goddess Ashtoreth was associated with war and fertility. Baal-Zebul, thought to be Dagon's son, was worshiped at Ekron.

Topic C: Samson — Set Apart for God

1. Describe the circumstances of Samson's miraculous birth. (See Judges 13:1–14, 24–25.)

2. Describe what each of the following passages says about what it means to be a Nazirite:

   a. Numbers 6:1–3

   b. Numbers 6:4

   c. Numbers 6:5

   d. Numbers 6:6–7

   e. Numbers 6:8

   f. Numbers 6:9–12

Topic D: Samson and the Philistines—Confrontation and Compromise

1. Samson sought opportunities to confront the Philistines. What was his intent in each of the following encounters?

Judges 14:1–4	
Judges 15:1–5	
Judges 15:9–15	

2. In what ways did Samson violate his Nazirite vow and compromise his calling?

   a. Numbers 6:6–7; Judges 14:5–9

   b. Numbers 6:4; Judges 14:10

   c. Judges 16:1–3

Topic E: God Uses Failure to Accomplish His Purposes

1. What were the short-term and long-term consequences of Samson's relationship with Delilah, a Philistine woman living in the Sorek Valley?

Short-term Consequences	Long-term Consequences
Judges 16:5, 16–21	Judges 16:23–30

2. Clearly God can use human failure and weakness to accomplish His purposes. Describe the weaknesses of the following people and how God used them.

    a. Moses (See Exodus 3:9–11; 4:1, 10–16; 33:12–17.)

    b. David (See 2 Samuel 11:1–5, 14–17; 12:24.)

    c. Peter (See Luke 22:54–62; John 21:15–19.)

faith lesson

Time for Reflection

Please read the following passage of Scripture silently and take the next few minutes to reflect on the ways in which God would have you confront the culture of your world.

> Some time later, he [Samson] fell in love with a woman in the Valley of Sorek whose name was Delilah. The rulers of the Philistines went to her and said, "See if you can lure him into showing you the secret of his great strength and how we can overpower him so we may tie him up and subdue him. Each one of us will give you eleven hundred shekels of silver." . . .
>
> Having put him to sleep on her lap, she called a man to shave off the seven braids of his hair, and so began to subdue him. And his strength left him.
>
> Then she called, "Samson, the Philistines are upon you!"
>
> He awoke from his sleep and thought, "I'll go out as before and shake myself free." But he did not know that the LORD had left him.
>
> Then the Philistines seized him, gouged out his eyes and took him down to Gaza. Binding him with bronze shackles, they set him to grinding in the prison. . . .
>
> Now the rulers of the Philistines assembled to offer a great sacrifice to Dagon their god and to celebrate, saying, "Our god has delivered Samson, our enemy, into our hands."
>
> When the people saw him, they praised their god, saying, "Our god has delivered our enemy into our hands, the one who laid waste our land and multiplied our slain."
>
> While they were in high spirits, they shouted, "Bring out Samson to entertain us." So they called Samson out of the prison, and he performed for them.
>
> When they stood him among the pillars, Samson said to the servant who held his hand, "Put me where I can feel the pillars that support the temple, so that I may lean against them." Now the temple

was crowded with men and women; all the rulers of the Philistines were there, and on the roof were about three thousand men and women watching Samson perform. Then Samson prayed to the LORD, "O Sovereign LORD, remember me. O God, please strengthen me just once more, and let me with one blow get revenge on the Philistines for my two eyes." Then Samson reached toward the two central pillars on which the temple stood. Bracing himself against them, his right hand on the one and his left hand on the other, Samson said, "Let me die with the Philistines!" Then he pushed with all his might, and down came the temple on the rulers and all the people in it. Thus he killed many more when he died than while he lived.

JUDGES 16:4–5, 19–21, 23–30

1. In light of Samson's lusty willfulness, what change in attitude is evident in his final prayer to God? What was the result of his prayer?

2. Samson clearly had many faults, yet God used him to challenge the Philistines' power. Consider a time in your life when God used your weakness, or that of other people, as an opportunity to demonstrate His strength. What difference can God make in your life now, even when you feel inadequate to face a difficult challenge?

3. Which sinful aspects of modern culture are attractive to you? Wealth? Pleasure? Gratification? Recognition? What might you do to stand firm when you are tempted to compromise God's values?

4. God gave Samson a mission—to overcome the power of evil that was threatening His people. In what way(s) is the mission God has given you similar to that of Samson?

Action Points

The key points of this session are outlined below. Consider each point and jot down an action step (or steps) that you will commit to this week as a result of what you have learned today.

1. *As God's people, we—like Samson and the tribe of Dan— are called to be part of the confrontation between God and the ungodliness of the world.* Our calling is to live on the front lines—in our equivalent of the Shephelah, the place where opposing values clash—in order to confront secular values and influence the world for God. But we can only live out a God-centered lifestyle if we refuse to adopt the ungodly values of our culture. Thus we are to remain distinct from the world's culture, not to compromise with it.

Which aspects of your culture do you believe God would have you confront?

In what ways might you be trying to avoid the battles instead of "living in the Shephelah"—the place where God's values meet the pagan practices of your culture?

In what ways have you compromised with ungodly values around you and weakened the impact God wants you to make instead of being "set apart" for Him and His purposes?

2. *When God calls us to accomplish a specific task, it is essential that we complete it fully.* If we don't, then we—like the tribe of Dan that failed to chase the Philistines out of the land God had provided for His people—jeopardize the whole mission. But when we place all aspects of our lives under the dominion of God's value system and live in close relationship with Him, God will work through us! We can have a powerful impact. We can be like standing stones that represent God and His power to our culture.

What areas of your life have you not completely and distinctively committed to God and His way of life? What are you going to do about it?

If you were to apply the same kind of dedication to your personal mission as the Nazirites did during ancient times, how would your life be different?

ıron of culture

questions to think about

1. Think about a time when you were matched against a formidable opponent. Perhaps when you wanted a particular job but were not as qualified as other applicants. Perhaps when you were bidding for a contract but your company was not as large or well known as your competitors. Perhaps when you were treated unfairly and sought justice. Perhaps when your team had a 2–7 record and you faced a team with a 9–0 record. How did you feel in that situation?

2. When you find yourself in a difficult situation in which you feel insecure, how do you tend to respond?

video notes

Azekah
Pass over

Goliath represented Evil
9+ ft tall, 5000-6000 shekels armor
Philistine - Had iron   like scales

David Represented God -
Key to the battle - David wants the
world to know who God was.
He used what he was good at sling & rock

Using Our Gifts to Shape the "Iron" of Society

video Highlights

Note the map of Israel on page 82 and locate Azekah and Socoh. Note how far into the Shephelah Azekah is.

1. Why was what happened between David and Goliath in the Elah Valley so critical to the Israelites' survival?

   Irons

2. Goliath said to David, "Am I a dog that you come at me with sticks?" What did the video reveal about why David had primitive weapons?

   It's what he knew

3. If you had been an Israelite soldier, how might you have felt when you faced the weaponry of the Philistines—and the taunts of Goliath?

4. What finally enabled the Israelites to become a significant and influential power in their culture?

   They got the land God intended for them & the iron technology

Israel

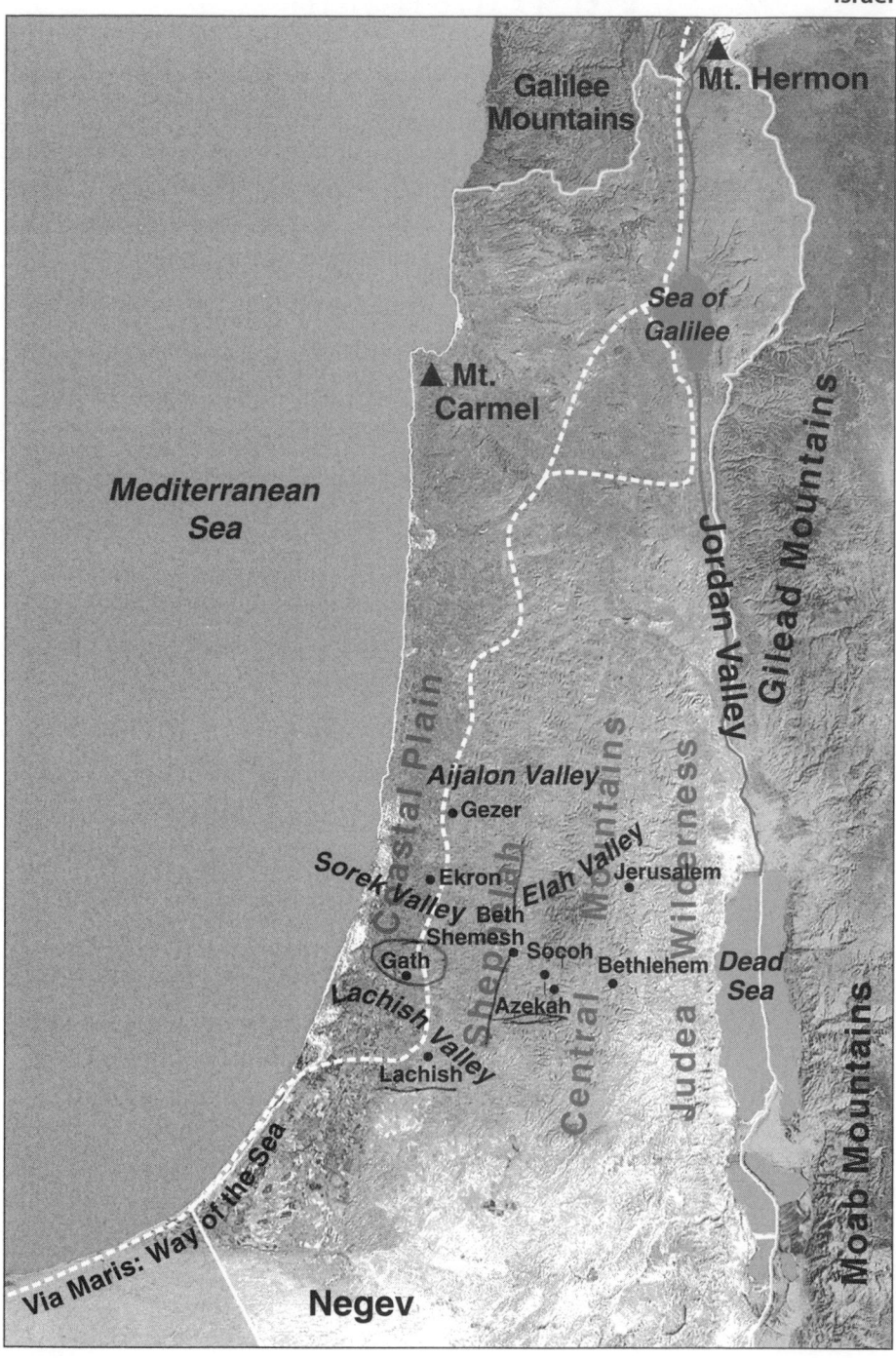

DATA FILE

Metalworking in the Middle East

Before 1200 B.C., bronze—a combination of copper and tin—was *the* metal used in the Middle East. Perhaps this was because the melting point of copper is 1,100 degrees Celsius and the melting point of iron is 1,550 degrees Celsius. Although bronze was a significant step beyond stone and wood, it was soft and didn't hold an edge well.

As the Bronze Age ended, many changes occurred. There were many invasions (both the Philistines and Israelites entered Canaan at this time), wars, and collapses of cultures. This resulted in a worldwide shortage of tin, which led to a scarcity of bronze.

During the thirteenth century B.C., an Aegean people—the Philistines— migrated to the Middle East. They may not have invented iron technology, but they used it effectively. In fact, they developed a process that included leaving iron in the fire long enough to absorb the carbon from firewood to form another more malleable form of iron—steel. This superior metal so revolutionized the world that it gave its name to the next 600 years—the Iron Age.

Iron, as a technological advancement during biblical times, could be compared to nuclear energy or computers today. It determined which cultures would dominate world events. It revolutionized how people lived—how much land they could plow, how much stone they could shape, how much wood they could cut. And it changed warfare greatly, just as gunpowder did centuries later.

The pagan Philistine culture dominated the Middle East during the early Iron Age, much as Western nations shape the cultures of developing nations today. The Philistines kept their iron technology secret so others could not use it. Since they lived on the coastal plain along the international trade route, they could also influence the world (a mission God had intended the Israelites to fulfill). The Israelites, on the other hand, did not even own swords and spears—and had to pay the Philistines to sharpen their tools (1 Samuel 13:19–22).

(continued on page 84)

(continued from page 83)

Between the time David killed Goliath and when he became king of Israel (2 Samuel 5), the Israelites learned the secret of iron technology and became the dominant culture (until they were unfaithful to God). Some scholars believe that David, or one of his people, learned this secret while living with the Philistines (1 Samuel 27–29). Although iron technology enabled David to destroy the enemies of God's people, he could not have been as successful as he was without God's hand upon him. Iron technology was one of the means by which God blessed David and provided a people, nation, and kingly pattern for the coming Son of David.

small group Bible Discovery

Topic A: A Clash of Cultures

The battle in the Elah Valley is significant not because David, a young shepherd who was untrained in warfare, defeated Goliath, a giant of a warrior, but because of what the battle represented.

1. Read 1 Samuel 17:1–3 and answer the following questions.

   a. Describe how the two armies positioned themselves for battle in the Shephelah region.

   b. Which army was the aggressor?

   c. Why was this an important battle for both sides?

2. Read 1 Samuel 17:4–7, 51 and describe the kind of warrior Goliath was.

3. Read 1 Samuel 17:5. What does the use of the word *scale* in describing Goliath's armor indicate?

4. Who, in effect, did Goliath defy when he made his loud challenges? (See 1 Samuel 17:10.)

5. What, in David's mind, was really at stake in the contest between him and Goliath? (See 1 Samuel 17:26, 45.)

CULTURES IN CONTRAST

Israelites	Philistines
Lived mainly in mountainous areas	Lived on the fertile coastal plain
Had primitive technology	Had advanced iron technology
Worshiped the one true God	Worshiped many gods through extremely immoral religious practices, including sacred prostitution

Topic B: The Battle Between God and Satan

Since the encounter in the Garden of Eden, the battle between God and Satan has been played out many times over in human history. Note the ways in which the writers of Scripture reveal their understanding of this battle through the events they record.

1. Read Genesis 3:14–15 and answer the following questions.

   a. What did God say would happen concerning the relationship between human beings and the devil and his seed?

   b. How would Satan's descendants be destroyed?

2. What is the parallel between Genesis 3:14–15 and the way in which Goliath died? (Read 1 Samuel 17:48–49.)

3. Read Daniel 3:1 and answer the following questions.

   a. How tall and wide was the statue in cubits?

   b. What do the numbers the writer used reveal about the true nature of this image?

c. Compare the height of Goliath in cubits (1 Samuel 17:4) with the dimensions of this statue. What does this reveal about Goliath's relationship to Satan?

4. Compare what God said in Deuteronomy 17:14–17 with 2 Chronicles 9:13, 15, 18, 25–28. What is the writer revealing about the moral quality of Solomon's wealth?

FACT FILE

Goliath

Philistine Armor

- Was a hardened warrior.
- Was more than nine feet tall.
- Wore a coat of bronze "scale" armor weighing 125 pounds. (The coat of mail was designed to protect its wearer without restricting movement.)
- Carried a spear that had a fifteen-pound point.
- Came from the Philistine city of Gath.
- Wore a bronze javelin on his back.
- Wore a bronze helmet.
- Defied the God of Israel ... and paid for it with his life.
- Symbolized evil, according to some scholars, who point to the ways in which the number six was used to describe him.

Topic C: The Battle Is Won

As the Israelite and Philistine armies faced one another in the Elah Valley, the great disparity in the quality of their military equipment was evident. Read the following references and compare the equipment of each.

	Philistines	Israelites	David
1 Samuel 13:19, 22			
1 Samuel 17:4–7			
1 Samuel 17:38–40			

2. What is significant about the way in which David approached the battle? (Read 1 Samuel 17:45–47.)

EVIDENCE FILE

Discoveries About Philistine Warriors

After finding carvings of Philistine soldiers in the temple of Ramses III in Egypt, archaeologists discovered that the soldiers:

- Wore feathered helmets secured under their chins by leather straps. Headbands, probably of metal, held the feathers in place.
- Wore breastplates and short skirts that had wide hems and tassels.
- Were clean shaven and quite tall.
- Sometimes carried small, round shields and straight swords.

3. God chose David and used his skill with the sling to gain victory. What does this demonstrate about the way in which God uses people—even their most simple talents—to accomplish His purposes?

4. Describe how each side responded to David's victory (1 Samuel 17:51–53).

   a. The Philistines:

   b. The Israelites:

Tel Azekah

Topic D: The Consequences of Disobedience—Saul's Failure to Fulfill God's Calling

1. How did King Saul respond to David's continued success in fighting the Philistines? (Read 1 Samuel 18:5–9, 12–16, 20–21, 24–25.)

2. Early in the Israelites' history, what did God command the Israelites to do? (Read Deuteronomy 25:17–19.)

3. Years later, whom did God choose to destroy the Amalekites? (Read 1 Samuel 15:1–3.)

4. What did Saul do to the Amalekites? (Read 1 Samuel 15:7–10.)

5. About 400 years later, what did Haman—a descendant of Agag—plan to do to all the Jews? (Read Esther 3:1–11.) If Haman had done this, what would have happened to God's plan of salvation?

6. What is significant about Esther's family heritage, and how did God use her to save the Jews? (Read 1 Samuel 9:1–2; Esther 2:5–7, 17; 6:1–10; 7:1–7, 9; 9:5–10.)

Topic E: Choosing God's Ways or the World's Ways

Solomon was the wisest king who ever lived. Yet in many ways he failed to obey God. In so doing, he allowed the world's culture to shape him rather than using his gifts to influence the culture for God.

1. God provided clear instructions for those who would be king over His people. Compare the following commands with Solomon's response.

God's Command	Solomon's Response
Deuteronomy 17:16:	2 Chronicles 9:25, 28:
Deuteronomy 17:17a:	1 Kings 11:1–3:
Deuteronomy 17:17b:	2 Chronicles 9:13–14, 27:

2. The wisest human king who ever lived failed to obey God and thus fell short of his calling. But there is another king who described himself as "one greater than Solomon."

   a. Who is He? (See Matthew 12:42.)

b. What is His all-consuming purpose? (See Matthew 18:11; Luke 22:39–42; John 4:34; 14:8–13; 1 Timothy 2:5–6.)

faith Lesson

Time for Reflection

Please read the following passage of Scripture silently and take the next few minutes to reflect on what the battle between David and Goliath was all about.

> Goliath stood and shouted, . . . "This day I defy the ranks of Israel! Give me a man and let us fight each other." On hearing the Philistine's words, Saul and all the Israelites were dismayed and terrified. . . .
>
> David said to Saul, "Let no one lose heart on account of this Philistine; your servant will go and fight him."
>
> Saul replied, "You are not able to go out against this Philistine and fight him; you are only a boy, and he has been a fighting man from his youth."
>
> But David said to Saul, "Your servant has been keeping his father's sheep. When a lion or a bear came and carried off a sheep from the flock, I went after it, struck it and rescued the sheep from its mouth. When it turned on me, I seized it by its hair, struck it and killed it. Your servant has killed both the lion and the bear; this uncircumcised Philistine will be like one of them, because he has defied the armies of the living God. The LORD who delivered me from the paw of the lion and the paw of the bear will deliver me from the hand of this Philistine." . . .
>
> David said to the Philistine, "You come against me with sword and spear and javelin, but I come against you in the name of the LORD Almighty, the God of the armies of Israel, whom you have defied. This day the LORD will hand you over to me, and I'll strike you down

and cut off your head. Today I will give the carcasses of the Philistine army to the birds of the air and the beasts of the earth, and the whole world will know that there is a God in Israel. All those gathered here will know that it is not by sword or spear that the LORD saves; for the battle is the LORD's, and he will give all of you into our hands."

1 SAMUEL 17:8, 10–11, 32–37, 45–47

1. How do the motives David had in challenging Goliath (17:45–46) apply to Christians today who are called to challenge the evils of our culture?

2. David recognized that the battle with Goliath was God's battle, not his battle. How does that belief empower you to use your gifts and talents to confront evil in your culture?

3. When David stepped out in faith and used his skills for God, the Israelite soldiers regained confidence in themselves and God and won a great victory. How might you encourage and influence your family or friends for God by stepping out in faith to promote God and His values? Think of a situation in which you could stand up for the Lord and encourage other people.

4. When David killed Goliath, the Philistine soldiers saw the power of God at work and ran away. How might people respond to you when you step forward in faith and use your skills and talents in God's service?

Action Points

Please take the next few moments to review the lessons of the battle between David and Goliath. Consider how those lessons apply to your life and make a commitment to take action because of what you have learned.

1. *God can use people who seem to have little to offer to accomplish His purposes.* When we seek to accomplish God's work, our motivation and faith in God is far more significant than our talent or resources. David, for example, was a young shepherd who appeared to have little to offer, but he acted as God's representative. He used his training and primitive tools in order to reveal the God of Israel to the world of his day. He used a simple sling to throw a stone at a man who had the best military technology an advanced culture could offer—and he triumphed because God honored his throw.

   Which gifts or talents, no matter how insignificant they may seem from a human viewpoint, are you willing to use to accomplish God's work?

2. *God wants each of us to use our particular gifts and talents to influence our culture for Him.*

   David did what God had qualified and gifted him to do, and because David was motivated by righteousness, he made a powerful impact on his culture. Likewise, we don't have to be anything other than the people God has created us to be in order to accomplish His purposes. Who He has made us to be is good enough. We need only to express the gifts and talents He has given us.

In what way(s) can you use your gifts and talents to honor God and influence the culture around you? Be specific.

3. *God wants us to use every resource, including the tools and technology of our culture—its "iron"—to accomplish His purposes.* The Israelites achieved a decisive victory over the Philistines when David killed Goliath. Unfortunately, the Philistines remained the superior culture for quite a while afterward (1 Samuel 31). Only when the Israelites, under the reign of faithful King David, harnessed the Philistines' advanced iron technology and used it for God's purposes did they become a great influence and power. Today, Christians who hold a Bible-based value system and are able to shape and control the "iron" aspects of their society will greatly impact their culture.

Which technologies that are shaping the culture of our society—its "iron," so to speak—can you impact for God while remaining faithful to the standards He has set for you? (The field of law? Politics? Education? Journalism? Movie production? Community?)

How could you support others who help shape the iron of our culture?